Wallace, Idaho

Idaho Wallace

Linda L. Beeman

World Enough Writers

Poetry
ISBN 978-1-937797-01-0

Cover photo by Linda L. Beeman
Author photo by Michael Stadler

Book and Cover Design by Tonya Namura
using Portland and Gill Sans

World Enough Writers
c/o Lana Ayers
PO Box 1808
Kingston, WA 98346

WorldEnoughWriters@gmail.com

Website: http://worldenoughwriters.com

In loving memory of my parents,
Leona and Bob Hall

Contents

Idaho Wallace

Galena

in the beginning is galena
lead sulfide crystallized
brittle as glass
heavy as guilt

housing silver lead zinc
at its core   puzzling
their way out to the world
compromised along the way

Wallace, Idaho

how to tell this story
a small town profiting
and despoiled
by another extraction industry

Cripple Creek   Deadwood   Smelterville
countless examples loiter
at the end of derelict roads
proving that money—
like warm air   rises

what kind of place is this
a drive-by tourist asked the woman at the front desk
can you imagine
she confided in me
returning native daughter

imagining is easy for most
viewing this hard edge
bastion of not-surrendering-to-quaint

not while dreams of more silver—
a mother lode   lurk deep below
as above   Lead Creek runs
rowdily through it

Extraction

is a chilling word
redolent of dentist chairs
high-pitched drills   the crack
of tooth wrenched from bone

underground ore mining
requires larger violence
pneumatic jackdrills bite into rock face
spit automatic gunfire staccato

hot dark dangerous
work of men wired for risk
how much do starting miners make—
I asked our guide

$9.20 an hour   he said
if you can find the work
that could be for owners careless
of safety   prudent with expenditure

Lucky Friday, Sunshine, Bunker
Hill, Star-Morning and Galena
hopeful names echo in my memory—
through a carbon monoxide fog
that suffocated 91 men at Sunshine

resource extraction consumes people
deep in the earth Orpheus seeks silver
forgets where he last saw Eurydice

On the Rocks

by 1955 only weathered screeds
painted on the odd boulder
denouncing Wobblies survived
hinting at savage battles—
union versus mine owner

1892 saw miners striking to protest
hourly pay cuts to 30 cents
dynamiting mills taking scabs hostage seizing mines
federal troops rounded up 600 men
bull-penned them for 60 days without charge

Bunker Hill's concentrator was the next target
blown to hell in 1899
black federal troops arrived   arrested
every man in Burke   loaded them
into boxcars for the ride to their corral

Idaho's governor   gifted with a bomb
for his contribution to preserving that peace
died mangled within the hour
his assassin confessed that
union bosses gave the order

we didn't learn this in our history classes
no martial law   no Pinkerton spies—
no desperate arrests   only graffiti messages
painted on rocks   daring us to find out why

Coeur d'Alene

all my life growing up
in the Coeur d'Alenes
I thought I lived in a place
called *heart of the owl*

no French speaker   I
was downcast to learn
the real meaning
heart of an awl

bestowed by a disgruntled
French-Canadian trader who
got the short end in a transaction
with a local native

no poetry in that name
bitter at its core
but there is a ring to the syllables
tri-part music in its soul

so I forgive him the meanness
and sing *core da lane*
imagining my home's avatars
silent-winged raptors

August 1910

a fire before my memory
flung itself down creek canyons
blacked skies   sucked oxygen
from the air   created tornados
knocked down hillsides of trees

only months before a new forest service
sent Yale graduates west   each
responsible for half a million wilderness
acres   novice administrators
one of whom cabled to headquarters

two undesirable prostitutes established
on government land   what should I do—
get two desirable ones came the reply
their attractions irrelevant now
as inferno leapt from tree to tree

panic palpable as static electricity
stood your hair to attention
asphyxiating as the fear
of not knowing how to escape
or if it was possible

fire was a feral animal
searching for fuel   your
house   your body   the wood
trestles under railway tracks
bridging ravines that offered a way out

run east   west   find a cave
flatten yourself in a creek   risk the train

after   amid charred ruins
silver still glinted down in the dark
a chastened Wallace rebuilt
itself in brick and stone

Lead Creek

fear of a fast running river—
babies swept away in taupe waters
tinted with cadmium arsenic cyanide

our mothers thought we would
drown in Lead Creek   vanish
forever in the smelter runoff

one early fall morning a riderless
pack horse trotted by my balcony bedroom
my horse I rejoiced   having longed lifetimes for one

no time to dress   I set off in pajamas
down Bank Street up King   but could not keep up
my thwarted need compounded by the scolding
about disappearing and likely being
immersed in a torrent of tailings

each summer fraternal organizations
sponsored the Lead Creek Derby
a beach ball dropped into the water at Mullan—
timed as it crossed the finish line in Wallace
nightmare shape-shifted into civic fundraiser

we'll bet on us we said to face down
pollution   power   fear
fireworks and parades
children on tricycles with crepe paper
woven through wheel spokes

floats with pretty girls in prom dresses
waving graciously from chicken wire thrones
stopped traffic on US 10

Halloween

in Wallace night came quick and black
oil slicks skimmed puddles
frost sliced the air
snow slush might melt in gutters

we roamed loose   parentless
free to knock on any door
no thought of razors or abduction
children in charge   giggling in the dark

each door promised treasure
Hershey's chocolate   raisinettes
nothing was outside our grasp
even magnate Harry Magnuson's door

loomed large and full of promise
until my mother said I should ring
our pastor's bell, say *trick or treat—*
but this year the treat's on me

and offer him my chocolate

that story made his Sunday sermon
but I never quite forgave her

Hook Houses

every 12-year-old charged
with selling something to benefit anything
knew   like the Lord's Prayer
the first steps you climbed led to brothel doors

soft hearts and canny calculations resided
at the Oasis, Lux and Sahara
yielding huge profits for fresh
faces with good causes to support

over the years we appeared with crayon
colored flags stapled to straws   only a nickel
then chocolate candy bars
Wallace High School emblazoned on the wrappers

my classmate Bruce realized
their potential   knocked earnestly
pleaded our cause
we always won most-money-raised contests
didn't imagine complicity in consequence

we need the houses mothers told daughters
they protect us from lust run amok
so many reckless young men
with testosterone to burn

city officials liked them too
for tax revenues   for the police cruiser
they donated to the community

the houses taught so many life lessons
how to confront the terror of sex
what gains strange bedfellows can realize
the value of old-fashioned hypocrisy

Huckleberries

stained our summers
dyed our tongues deep purple
smeared our picking fingers red

Shirley and I drove to Moon Pass
on hot August mornings
tin pails hanging from strings
around our necks   excited

about the killing we would make
when we visited the Smokehouse
that evening   selling our berries
for the extravagant price of $8
a gallon

Storm King

drawing that mountain
outside our window
again and again
etched it in my mind

not the most magnificent
peak in the Bitterroots
but my mountain

simple wide inverted V
a woman's legs
where I hiked through wild syringa

where I chased a runaway horse
where Ed Pulaski and his men
hid in a cave from that furious fire

like writing your name
over a lifetime
the repetition of lines
shapes you as you shape them

fifty years later I could still
make a fair representation
was confounded when   coming home
it wasn't guarding our house

a ghost that should have been there
you know how mountains can be
mirages on their horizons

my mountain had not moved for me
simply hid behind evergreens
grown taller since childhood
seen lower now from sidewalks

Delores

was madam at the Lux Rooms
drove a pink Cadillac and dyed her hair
alarming colors   strode the street
with a guilt's-not-for-me gait

egg timers at every institution
signaled when your money was spent
business was business after all
everyone knew that

captain of our drill team
we marched   shoulders back   heads high
in parades wearing red sweaters with black Ws
center front   for Wallace
white boots red tasseled   not W for whore

shrill whistle notwithstanding
adolescent taunts greeted us everywhere
chanting *we wanna W*

Timothy said he grew up on the wrong
side of Spokane where Wallace meant one thing
in dead winter he drove with friends
knocked on a door and was greeted

by a woman smoking a cigarette
dangling a long ash
wearing a one-piece bathing suit
with high heels
asking   *What'll it be boys*

he said they ran like hell

White

pinpricks of white come down
faster and closer every hour
roads close   temperatures drop
signaling *you are on your own*

hallways of shoveled snow
twice my height enclosed me as I walked
to school   snow canyons   snow mazes
in quantities and weights that collapsed roofs

never earned us school closures
allowed banks or government offices
to shut or miners the day off

sledding down High Street through
ice ruts one afternoon sent me
straight into the iron fence post
that broke my forehead

and direct to hospital for stitches
needle through flesh   as calamitous
a thought as those inoculation clinics
my mother presided over

snow stifles sound   lies serene
but underneath that pristine blanket
lurks isolation   cold   black ice
that skids us into God only knows

Leona

was the school nurse
my mother not only conducted
inoculation clinics   she tested
our eyes   our ears   my moral mettle

gregarious in her Norwegian
way   loving the outdoors
skiing   community of church
singing loudly in a quavering alto

she savored warm taste of *lefse*
with butter and cheese
a longing I inherited

when a showdown came over
religion   I said I couldn't believe
she told me it felt like
I'd slapped her face

but when I confessed my 20-year
marriage had ended she said
she'd never liked him anyway

when I was seven we made a bargain—
she'd pay a dollar for every book I read
and wrote a report about   how could she
imagine James Baldwin

or the gift she'd given me

The Mission

Idaho's oldest building   a benediction
overlooking Coeur d'Alene Lake
where steamers disembarked
miners from the coast

Jesuit friar Ravalli
carved reverence
into it with his pocket knife

native converts shaped its mud
straw walls with their hands
their prints still visible today

their better worlds
meshed so squarely
native with Catholic
burnt sage with incense
shaman with saint

Cataldo's snipped-tin chandeliers pendant
from baroque folk-painted ceilings
beacons above Coeur d'Alene River

where mining toxins bled into the lake
decimating livestock   *leaded horses*
leaded cows farmers called them
poisoning alighting tundra swans

Flight

I couldn't wait to get away
volunteered to attend Catholic
high school in Spokane
not my faith, but a life valve

there were moments in the 60s—
when I saw *Breakfast at Tiffanys*
when I read *A Fire Next Time*—
stunning episodes that prompted

my mother to ask why a call girl
was so attractive and me to write
Mr. Baldwin   assuring him
he had a friend in Wallace

constriction tight as a cross
your heart bra   left me
sitting alone in an Oakland dorm room
breathless   terrified

thought I could write checks
deposit them to my account
boost my balance   then fly to LA
see Johnny Carson

everything was possible
now that I was out

May 1972

past the golf course up Big Creek
down underground shafts and tunnels
an ordinary day at Sunshine Mine

where miners blasted and mucked out
year after year sending
ore out in rail cars at treadmill
pace to the refining smelter

on that day a fire sent acrid smoke
slithering down shafts and through raises

everyone knew rock didn't burn
so few were alarmed   a mistake
this time when carbon monoxide
reached levels that killed in two breaths

found later   their bodies caught
inhaling the third
one man chewed a sandwich
another lit a cigarette

none recognizable except by tattoos
jewelry   some had to be pick-axed
releasing gases for recovery

Ron Flory and Tom Wilkinson emerged
after sheltering for a week
at 4800 in a vented safety zone
but went uncelebrated

they'd been Sunshine shills
dead miner's wives said
Flory an addict, Wilkinson a drunk
how could they survive and not my husband—

conjecture turned dark and mean
as the stopes and raises yielded 91 corpses

later in a bar a widow slapped
Flory's face   hard   for the sin of having lived
while her husband rotted

In the Box

superfund is an odd word
suggesting silver heaped chests
investment banker excess

but that wealth migrated further afield
leaving contaminated soils
fouled wetlands saturated with heavy metals
in an area called the Bunker Hill box

over a century 100 million tons of waste
worked their way into rivers without fish
backyards where children did not play
mountains bald of white pine

black slag heaps welcomed visitors
from the west to our Silver Valley
like upside down orcas in winter
when snow capped the tailings

cleaning catastrophes like ours consumes
decades   costs billions   bankrupted ASARCO
coins new words like repository
secure places where contaminated soils are disposed

ours   East Mission Flats   is in the box
part of the larger basin   rectangles
within rectangles and layers beneath layers
poisoned geometries

I-90

who would have imagined Wallace—
cedar swamp hugging the south fork
of the Coeur d'Alene—
could withstand federal pressure

to replace US-10   running I-90's
machete through our torso
bisecting our brick built-to-last center
demolishing our heart so east-west
traffic could briskly do its business

who after all
wants to be detained by history

that question   *what kind of place is this*
captures curiosity about a town
without strip malls or national branding
a broken place with its head
just above Lead Creek

eminent domain coerced every merchant
into a national historic district listing
Harry Magnuson sued the state department
of transportation   the federal highway
administration that   in its haste to buy
rights-of-way inadvertently purchased a brothel

they stopped the bulldozers
repositioned an old railway station
channeled Lead Creek
rappelled a new interstate north above town
like a ski jump over Wallace

Harry

lived down the block at First and Bank
grandson of one of those bull penned
miners caught up in early labor wars

born in Wallace yet looking outside
our Bitterroots he found wider worlds
the Navy   then a Harvard MBA

Wallace drew him back and mining
offered a way forward   not
on a direct route   *he danced and did battle*

with local companies over decades
his accounting and penny stock savvy
built inroads and a fortune

he won that suit against Sunshine
that included a seven-figure annual payment
provided he never entered their office again

good Catholic boy   shrewdness coupled
with sentiment in him   he guaranteed
Gonzaga University's debts   enabled its survival
quietly bankrolled college educations

preserved Idaho's oldest building
the Cataldo Mission
and rescued Wallace from an interstate's maw

R. G.

my father was a careful man
regular in his habits
off in the morning to keep ASARCO's books
back in the evening to watch the news
smoke a pipe in his swivel chair

he guarded his neat green lawn with an air gun
instructing neighborhood dogs
not to linger in our yard

we went for drives in our '54 Plymouth
maintained deliberate speeds to the IGA
where we earned S&H Green Stamps
pasted them into books for redemption

after marriage I came home
dragging my big city husband behind me
first real collision between Josiah
and my small town parents

four days into our visit, needing a break
Joe said he'd walk to the grocery
R.G. pulled the Plymouth out

said *No trouble* and off they went
on their six block errand   returned
three hours later   husband exasperated

Daddy parked in the empty
grocery lot as far from the entrance
as he could   turned off the engine
said *On sunny days like this elk come out
on that mountain over there*

they sat in silence for two and a half hours
before my father acknowledged
Guess they're not coming today

Ag

silver is a subtle metal
not as flashy as gold
elusive as platinum
light as titanium

native jewelry floats to mind
along with tea services
the tang of fork tines
substantial reassurance

I recall the heft of silver dollars
in teenage purses
heavy as book bags

photographic chemicals and dental
amalgams snag our notice
but we probably don't realize

its antiseptic properties or its slick
thermal and electric conductivity—
broken into atomic dimensions
nanosilver combats microbes

battles body odor
struggles with sepsis
in washing machines   dietary supplements
toothpaste   catheters and condoms

it coats our clothing
sanitizes food and beverage containers
silver lurks in unexpected places
winking just beneath the surface

Miners

unhinge me
their raw edginess a glimpse
into hot dark underground

ignorance is the price those of us
who don't descend are glad to pay
nice to have a glinting bauble
rare earth powering our e-device

those 91 asphyxiated at Sunshine
remind us this is hard mean work
fear and adrenalin mix down there
dripping heat back-grounded with

drilling   blasting   mining   music
hard rock with a heavy metal beat
that stands your hairs on end

Return

over mountain pass   across wind-scoured Columbia
back in time to a childhood home
raw with jagged edge
chip-on-the-shoulder bluff
hiding decades of hope grasped
then lost with open-fist abandon

the mother lode said our guide
had been found two miles
down under the valley
now mines would reopen
in this latest silver rush

money and booze and whores
would gush from the earth
like last time   before capital
siphoned west to Spokane, east to New York
elusive as a vanished ore vein
that cracked flaw in the rock

metal still glints from down in the dark
and flames in our mind's eye
the flaw is the thing we love

Acknowledgments

I began to mistrust that $9.20 per hour salary our mining tour leader gave me and contacted Hecla Mining Company in May, 2011 to see what they pay miners without prior experience. According to Sara Brashier, Compensation and Benefits Administrator for Hecla, the entry level rate for their Wallace mine is $15.49 per hour.

The Forest Service message about undesirable prostitutes appears in Elers Koch's *Forty Years a Forester*. Missoula: Mountain Press Publishing, 1998.

My thanks to Scott Reed for taking the time to speak with me about the suit against the Idaho State Department of Transportation and the Federal Highway Administration mentioned in the poem "I-90."

Thanks as well to John Magnuson, Harry's son, who read the three poems that mention Harry and thought they tilted too far toward money. I can only say I'm not an historian or a psychiatrist. Just a poet.

Harry 'danced and did battle' according to an obituary titled "Community Activist Magnuson Dies at 85" by David Bond published in the *Shoshone News Press* of January 26, 2009.

I would give much to have written the final line in "Return," *the flaw is the thing we love*, but I didn't. It nearly floored me while I was reading Gail Caldwell's *Let's Take the Long Way Home: A Memoir of Friendship*. New York: Random House, 2010.

~

Delores was awarded first prize for poetry in the age 25+ category by the Bend, OR *Nature of Words* "Rising Star" competition in 2011.

White was published in the Spring 2012 issue of *Pinyon*, a journal published by Colorado Mesa University, Grand Junction, CO.

R.G. was published on-line at the *Adanna* Web site for the April 15, 2012 themed page of Fathers/Daughters.

May 1972 was published in the Spring, 2012 issue of *Windfall*.

About the Author

Linda Beeman is an award-winning non-fiction writer and poet living on Whidbey Island in Puget Sound. Her poems have been published in *Windfall: A Journal of Poetry and Place*, Colorado Mesa University's *Pinyon* and online at *Adanna* and the University of Chicago's *Euphony*.

Her exploratory travel articles appeared in *The Los Angeles Times* and *The Foreign Service Journal*.

She researches and writes extensively about antique textiles from South and Southeast Asia and believes curiosity extends the cat's life.

Made in the USA
Charleston, SC
29 December 2012